MAYER SMITH

Frosted Souls and Fiery Hearts

Contents

One

A Kingdom of Ice

The wind howled like a wounded beast, carrying shards of ice through the jagged peaks of the Frostlands. Princess Seraphina stood at the highest balcony of the royal palace, her pale fingers resting against the stone railing as she gazed at the approaching entourage. A long line of banners fluttered against the wind—deep crimson, the color of blood and fire, bearing the sigil of the Ember Empire. They had arrived.

She inhaled slowly, drawing the cold into her lungs, letting it settle in her chest like a second heartbeat. Her entire life had been defined by frost, by the weight of expectation, by the prophecy whispered in dark corridors—the one that claimed fire and ice should never meet, lest they consume the world in their battle.

And yet, here she was. Betrothed to a man she had never met.

Her fingers curled into a fist, and a thin layer of frost bloomed over the railing. She released the tension, watching the ice crack and fall away.

The heavy doors behind her creaked open.

"You should not be out here," came a voice, sharp as a blade but softer beneath its edge. It was Queen Elira, her mother. She stepped forward, her silver gown shifting like flowing ice, her hair, the same pale shade as Seraphina's, braided in an intricate coil. "They will see you before you see them. A queen should not reveal herself so easily."

Seraphina did not turn. "I am not a queen."

"Not yet." A pause. "But soon."

Seraphina closed her eyes. The word felt like a chain around her throat. Soon, she would be bound to a man from a kingdom that had been their enemy for centuries. Soon, she would leave the Frostlands for a place where fire burned the sky, where the air tasted of cinders instead of snow. Soon, she would be expected to love a man who could unmake her with a single touch.

She opened her eyes. The procession had entered the palace gates.

"I am ready," she said, though the words tasted like ice on her tongue.

Queen Elira studied her for a long moment before nodding. "Then let us welcome your future."

The grand hall was alight with the glow of enchanted lanterns, but Seraphina felt only the cold. The frost in her veins, the storm in her heart. The Ember royals stood at the far end of the chamber, their presence an open flame against the stark whites and blues of the Frostlands.

She barely heard the formal introductions. Her focus had narrowed to one man.

Prince Kael.

He stood at the center of the delegation, taller than she expected, his presence like the ember of a dying fire—controlled, waiting, but capable of roaring into an inferno at any moment. His black hair, tousled by the wind, framed a face carved with sharp angles, his skin bronzed by the heat of his kingdom's endless sun. But it was his eyes that unsettled her.

A deep, smoldering gold. Like molten fire. Like something that could burn through her if she dared to get too close.

Seraphina lifted her chin, forcing herself to meet his gaze without faltering. If he expected to see fear, he would be disappointed.

His lips quirked into something that wasn't quite a smirk, but close enough to make her pulse tighten.

"A pleasure to finally meet you, Princess," he said, his voice smooth, but laced with something unreadable. "I've heard much about you."

Her heartbeat was steady. Slow. She would not let him see her nerves. "I wish I could say the same, but I know little of you, Prince Kael."

"Then allow me to make a proper introduction." He took a step closer, bridging the space between them. The moment he did, something shifted in the air.

The warmth of his presence wrapped around her, foreign and unrelenting. Seraphina stiffened as a strange sensation coiled through her, her magic reacting—no, recoiling. Ice and fire, forced into the same space, neither willing to yield.

For a fraction of a second, she thought she saw a flicker of something in his expression—an awareness, a recognition of whatever had just passed between them.

He extended a gloved hand, waiting. A test.

She knew that accepting it would set the tone for what came next. A queen should not reveal herself so easily.

And yet, she did.

The moment her fingers met his, the world shifted.

A hiss of steam curled between their joined hands. Seraphina inhaled sharply, barely suppressing the gasp that threatened to escape her lips. Heat licked at her skin, but it was not painful—it was unfamiliar. Kael's hand tensed beneath hers, as though he too had felt the pulse of something neither of them understood.

Her frost. His fire. Touching. Reacting. Fighting.

His gaze met hers again, and this time, there was no mistaking the flicker of intrigue. "Interesting," he murmured, his voice just low enough that only she could hear.

She forced herself to withdraw, her heart pounding against her ribs. The entire court was watching. They had seen nothing but a brief touch, an exchange of pleasantries. They did not feel what she had felt.

A danger. A warning.

She looked at Kael again, and something in his eyes told her that he had felt it too.

Later that night, long after the formalities had ended, Seraphina stood by her window, staring at the distant flames flickering in the Ember Empire's camp. She clenched her fingers, feeling the lingering warmth from his touch.

This was not a simple betrothal.

This was something else.

Something dangerous.

And something deep within her whispered—he would either be her ruin, or she his.

Two

A Cold Reception

The Frostlands Palace loomed like an untouched jewel—sharp, pristine, and merciless. The walls, sculpted from ice and stone, shimmered under the glow of enchanted lanterns, casting eerie reflections along the frozen corridors. Every breath Kael took felt like knives in his lungs, the bitter air unfamiliar, relentless.

He had expected the cold. He had prepared for it.

Yet, nothing could have truly braced him for the way it clung to him like an unwanted second skin, burrowing deep into his bones, whispering in a language of frost and silence. This place is not yours. You do not belong.

Prince Kael of the Ember Empire stood at the entrance of the grand dining hall, posture composed, his face schooled into calm indifference. The air crackled around him—not with warmth, but with an absence of it. It was the first time in his life he felt utterly out of his element. The flames within him dimmed, struggling to counter the oppressive chill.

At the head of the table, Princess Seraphina sat with the regal stillness of a queen, though she was not yet one. Her expression was unreadable, her pale-blue eyes the color of a frozen lake, deep and deadly.

She had barely spoken to him since their introduction.

Not that he expected warmth. He was fire, after all. And fire had no place here.

A servant passed him, offering a goblet of winterberry wine. He reached for it, but before his fingers could close around the cup, frost bloomed across its surface, creeping over the metal like skeletal fingers.

Kael's jaw tensed.

He glanced at Seraphina. She watched him over the rim of her glass, something unreadable in her gaze. A challenge. A test.

With slow deliberation, he lifted the goblet. The frost should have burned against his palm, but the moment he touched it, heat surged through his fingertips, melting the ice instantly. He took a long sip, never breaking eye contact with her.

Something flickered across her face—something sharp, like the edge of a dagger catching moonlight.

The moment passed as quickly as it came.

"So," Kael said, setting the goblet down, his voice cutting through the tension like a blade. "Shall we dispense with the pleasantries?"

A silence fell over the table. The nobles and courtiers, draped in furs and adorned with icy gemstones, turned their attention toward the two of them. Some curious, some wary.

Seraphina set her own goblet down, the soft clink echoing louder than it should have.

"I wasn't aware we had begun pleasantries," she said smoothly.

A smirk ghosted across his lips. She was not meek. He had suspected as much, but hearing it confirmed in her voice sent a strange thrill through him.

"Then let me be blunt," he continued, leaning forward slightly, letting his warmth inch toward her. "You don't want this union any more than I do."

A flicker of amusement. "That is a dangerous assumption, Prince Kael."

"You said yourself you know little of me."

"And yet, I know your kind." Her voice was softer now, but

no less sharp. "Your people worship the sun. They consume, conquer, burn." She tilted her head, regarding him with cool detachment. "Do you expect me to trust that you will not do the same here?"

Kael exhaled slowly. The weight of history hung between them.

The Ember Empire and the Frostlands had warred for centuries. Blood had been spilled, castles razed, kings and queens betrayed. The fragile truce between their nations rested on their shoulders now, bound by rings neither of them had yet worn.

He studied her, searching for a crack in that icy exterior. Was she afraid of him? Did she despise him? Or was there something else beneath her words—something more dangerous?

Before he could answer, the doors to the hall burst open.

A gust of frigid air rushed in, followed by a man clad in fur-lined armor. General Alric, commander of the Frostlands' armies. His eyes flickered toward Seraphina before landing on Kael with open distrust.

"My princess," Alric said, bowing low. "There has been an incident."

Seraphina's gaze darkened. "What kind of incident?"

Alric hesitated. "One that involves your betrothed."

A ripple of unease spread through the room. Kael felt the weight of a dozen stares pressing against him.

Seraphina rose, her movements fluid and deliberate. "Speak plainly, General."

Alric straightened. "One of our border outposts was set ablaze."

A chill crawled down Kael's spine, but it had nothing to do with the cold.

Seraphina turned to him, her expression unreadable once more. But this time, beneath the ice, there was suspicion.

"Are you accusing my people of breaking the truce?" Kael asked, voice calm but laced with steel.

Alric did not flinch. "I am saying that fire is not a weapon of the Frostlands."

The room grew impossibly colder.

Kael stood slowly, his fingers curling at his sides, heat simmering just beneath his skin. "And ice is not a weapon of my people, yet I've heard stories of Frostlanders who can freeze a man from the inside out." He held Seraphina's gaze. "Would you hold her accountable for every death caused by her kind?"

Alric bristled, but Seraphina lifted a hand, silencing him. She studied Kael carefully, her gaze unreadable. Then, after a long moment, she turned to Alric.

"Prepare my horse. I will go to the outpost myself."

"My princess—"

"This is my kingdom. And if someone seeks to divide it before this union has even begun, I will know why."

Kael watched her, intrigued. She did not immediately accuse him. She did not blindly accept the claims of her people.

She would investigate. She would see for herself.

And she would not leave him behind.

"I'm coming with you," Kael said.

A murmur rippled through the hall.

Seraphina arched a brow. "You wish to see the wreckage your people may have caused?"

He held her gaze, unwavering. "I wish to see the truth."

A silence stretched between them. A test. Another test.

Then, after a long pause, she nodded once.

"As you wish, Prince Kael."

The words were smooth, but Kael did not miss the slight shift in her tone—the smallest trace of warning.

Their fates were bound now. And whether this alliance would forge peace or ignite war was a question neither of them yet had an answer to.

13

Three

Secrets Beneath the Ice

The wind screamed through the desolate expanse of the Frostlands, carving through ice and stone as if seeking something long buried. It was a sound Kael was unaccustomed to—a mournful, eerie wail that whispered warnings in a language older than any kingdom.

He adjusted his grip on his stallion's reins, the beast's breath curling in the frozen air like smoke from a dying ember. Beside him, Seraphina rode with effortless grace, her cloak billowing behind her like a shard of the night sky. She had barely spoken since they left the palace, her focus trained ahead on the path to the burned outpost.

Silence suited her.

Kael had spent his life surrounded by voices—the crackling of flames, the roars of battle, the fervent chants of his people. He had grown accustomed to the warmth of noise, the weight of expectation in every spoken word. But Seraphina's silence was different. It was not absence. It was restraint.

And restraint, he knew, was far more dangerous.

They rode for hours, the landscape shifting from crystalline peaks to a frozen valley where the outpost once stood. Smoke still curled from its ruins, blackening the sky like a wound against the snow.

Kael dismounted, the heat in his blood stirring as he surveyed the wreckage. Fire had done this. But had it been his people's fire?

Seraphina walked ahead, her boots crunching over ice and ash. She knelt beside a shattered beam, brushing her gloved fingers over its charred surface. When she exhaled, a thin mist of frost seeped from her lips, weaving through the air like ghostly threads before dissipating.

She was testing something. He didn't know what.

"What do you see?" he asked.

She glanced at him, the flicker of a secret in her gaze. "The fire burned too quickly."

Kael frowned. "I don't follow."

She rose to her full height, brushing ash from her hands. "A normal fire spreads with the wind, devours slowly, leaves lingering embers. This fire…" She turned, her gaze sweeping the destruction. "It consumed everything in minutes. And then it died."

Kael knelt, pressing his hand against the blackened wood. The heat was long gone, the embers cold. She was right. A natural fire should have smoldered for days.

"This was not the work of ordinary flame."

Seraphina's lips pressed into a thin line. "Then whose flame was it?"

Kael stared at the ruins, feeling something stir in his chest—an unease he rarely entertained. This attack, this destruction… it felt wrong.

He exhaled slowly, allowing the warmth in his veins to pulse outward. The cold receded slightly, steam curling in the air. He focused, searching for remnants of magic, for traces of something left behind.

And then he felt it.

A pulse. Faint. Buried beneath the ruin, but unmistakable.

Magic.

Not fire magic.

Something older.

Seraphina moved suddenly, stepping past him toward what remained of the outpost's foundation. She crouched, pressing her hand to the ice. Kael felt it the moment she did. A shift in the air.

Then, before he could react—

A crack split through the silence.

The ice beneath them shattered.

Kael lunged, grabbing Seraphina's wrist as the ground gave way beneath them. The world spun into darkness, a tunnel of ice swallowing them whole.

They fell.

Kael hit the ground hard, the impact jolting through his spine. The air left his lungs in a sharp gasp, the cold biting into him like fangs. For a moment, he couldn't move.

Then he felt warmth.

Not his own.

Seraphina's body was pressed against his, her breath fanning over his jaw, her heartbeat a frantic rhythm against his chest.

He blinked, his vision adjusting to the dim glow of blue light surrounding them. Ice. They were beneath the outpost. Beneath the Frostlands.

Seraphina stirred, pushing herself up slightly. The movement brought them closer, their faces only inches apart. For a brief moment, neither of them spoke. The tension between them was thick, charged with something neither of them dared name.

Then she pulled away, rising to her feet.

Kael sat up, rubbing the back of his neck. "Well," he muttered. "That was a hell of a way to fall."

Seraphina ignored him, turning to survey their surroundings. The cavern was vast, its walls smooth and glistening with frost. But it was the center of the space that caught Kael's attention.

An altar.

Carved from ice and stone, its surface etched with markings he did not recognize. It pulsed faintly with blue light, the same magic he had sensed above.

Seraphina approached it slowly, her fingers tracing the runes. "I've seen these before," she murmured.

Kael stood, dusting himself off. "Where?"

She hesitated. "In the royal archives. In texts so old they are barely legible." Her voice grew softer, as if speaking too loudly would disturb something sleeping in the ice. "They spoke of a time before our kingdoms. Before fire and frost were divided."

Kael stepped beside her. "What did they say?"

Seraphina turned to face him, and for the first time since their meeting, he saw something flicker behind her guarded expression. Fear.

"They spoke of two forces that were never meant to be separated." She glanced back at the altar. "And of the destruction they would bring if they ever came together again."

A shiver ran down Kael's spine, but not from the cold.

Because in that moment, standing beside Seraphina, their magic thrumming in the air between them, he realized something.

The fire that destroyed the outpost was not an act of war.

It was a warning.

And he and Seraphina were standing right in the middle of it.

Four

The First Crack in the Ice

The palace halls had never felt colder. Despite the heavy tapestries draped over the walls and the roaring fire in the hearths, a chill seemed to seep into Kael's bones as he walked the corridors. It wasn't the Frostlands' relentless cold that gnawed at him now. It was the realization that he was caught in the middle of something far more dangerous than he had ever imagined.

His boots echoed on the stone floor, the rhythmic sound at odds with the thoughts swirling in his mind. A warning. The altar beneath the Frostlands had not been some relic of the past—it was a signal. A threat. But who had sent it?

And why was Seraphina involved?

He had hoped that the ride back to the palace would have

provided clarity, but instead, it had only deepened the questions in his mind. Seraphina had been quiet after they'd found the altar—too quiet. She had insisted they leave before anything else could happen, and despite the way her gloved fingers had trembled when she reached for his arm, she hadn't said a word since they returned to the palace.

Kael paused outside the grand doors to the royal chambers, where Seraphina had retreated to after their return. The corridors were nearly deserted, the silence pressing in on him like a physical weight. He reached for the door handle, hesitated, and then knocked.

There was no answer.

He knocked again, this time with a little more force, enough to break the stillness.

"Come in."

The voice came soft, distant, a faint thread of ice woven through the words. Kael pushed open the heavy door.

Seraphina stood by the window, her back to him, staring out at the snow-covered courtyard. The light from the moon danced over the icy landscape, casting shadows that seemed to move on their own.

He closed the door behind him, the sound of it clicking shut loud in the stillness.

"I thought I might find you here," he said, his voice steady despite the tightness in his chest.

She didn't turn. Instead, her fingers brushed against the frost on the windowpane, her breath fogging the glass as she exhaled.

"Why did you come?" she asked, her voice low, though there was an unmistakable edge to it now.

"Because I want answers."

Seraphina finally turned to face him. Her eyes, a pale blue like the deepest part of winter's night, were filled with a mixture of frustration and something else Kael couldn't place. Something sharp, but hidden behind layers of ice.

"You always want answers, don't you?" she said, her tone almost mocking. "Always searching for the truth, even when it's better left buried."

Kael's jaw clenched. "If you know something about what happened—about the altar, about the fire—now is the time to tell me."

Seraphina stepped forward, her movements graceful yet purposeful. She was like the frost itself—beautiful, but capable of freezing him in his tracks if he wasn't careful.

"There are things that you don't understand," she said softly, though there was a fire in her words now. "Things about this kingdom, about the power I wield. It's not just ice, Kael. There are forces at work here that neither of us can control."

He took a step closer, feeling the pull of her energy like a magnetic force. "You think I don't understand power?"

Her eyes flickered, the slightest spark of something—regret?—passing through them before it was quickly replaced by ice once again.

"No," she said, her voice a quiet challenge. "I think you understand your power. But not mine."

The silence between them stretched, thick and suffocating. Kael could feel the weight of her words pressing against him. There was so much she wasn't saying, so much hidden just beneath the surface.

"Tell me," he demanded, his voice softer now, though no less intense. "What aren't you telling me?"

Seraphina took a deep breath, as if bracing herself against the force of something she had been holding back for too long. "It's not just about us, Kael," she said, her voice tight. "This union, this… marriage between our kingdoms—there are forces beyond us, beyond what we understand, that are drawing us together. And they won't stop until…"

She faltered, her words hanging in the air like a whispered threat.

"Until what?" Kael pressed, stepping closer, his heart pounding in his chest.

She didn't answer immediately, but her gaze fell to the floor, the weight of her silence speaking volumes.

"They want us to fail," she whispered, almost to herself.

Kael's pulse quickened. "Who?"

Her eyes flickered up to meet his, the coldness in them now replaced by a flicker of fear. "I don't know yet."

The words hung in the air like smoke, dissipating slowly, leaving a trail of unanswered questions in their wake. The tension between them was thick, palpable. Kael's heart hammered in his chest as he realized that Seraphina wasn't just afraid of what was happening between them—she was afraid of what they were being forced into.

"I won't let anything happen to you," he said, his voice raw, though he barely recognized it as his own.

Seraphina took a step back, her eyes narrowing as she studied him. "You don't understand," she said, her voice a mix of frustration and something else, something softer. "I'm not the one you should be worried about."

Kael reached for her arm, but she pulled away, her breath catching slightly as if his touch had burned her. He didn't let go, his fingers tightening around her wrist, though he kept the pressure light, careful.

"I don't care who I should be worried about," he said, his voice low. "I care about you. We're in this together, whether you like it or not."

Seraphina's eyes flashed, and for the first time since they'd met, Kael saw the fire in her—the unspoken anger that had been smoldering just beneath the surface. She wrenched her arm away, stepping back with a sharp intake of breath.

"You think this is easy for me?" she snapped, her voice rising. "You think I want to be bound to a man who could burn me to ashes with a single touch? Or to a kingdom that's never known peace?"

Kael stood frozen for a moment, taken aback by the fierceness of her words. He had never seen this side of her—the side that wasn't cold, wasn't calculated.

And yet, in the space between them, something shifted. Something that neither of them could deny.

He stepped forward again, closing the distance between them. "I'm not your enemy, Seraphina. I'm here to protect you."

She looked up at him, her breath shallow, her eyes filled with a thousand emotions—fear, frustration, and a longing so deep it nearly cracked him open. For a brief, impossible moment, she didn't look like the princess of the Frostlands. She looked like a woman who, despite everything, was desperate for something more than what the world had offered her.

Before either of them could speak again, the door to the chamber swung open, breaking the moment.

"My princess."

A guard stood in the doorway, his expression grim. "There's been an attack on the western border. It's spreading quickly."

Seraphina's eyes flickered with something—something Kael couldn't place. He could almost see the decision form in her mind, like ice cracking beneath her feet.

"I'll be there," she said, her voice a mask once again, cold and commanding.

Kael opened his mouth to protest, to say something—anything—to stop her. But she was already gone, her figure disappearing into the shadows of the palace as quickly as she had appeared.

He stood there for a long moment, staring at the door, the silence echoing in his mind. They were not alone in this. Whoever—or whatever—was behind this conspiracy, Kael and Seraphina were its targets. And they were running out of time.

Five

Whispers of Rebellion

The night air was thick with the scent of burning wood. The smell of something more than just fire—a sharp tang of metal and oil, mixed with the scent of fear, filled Kael's senses. He rode at the head of the small contingent of soldiers sent by Seraphina to investigate the reports of a skirmish along the western border. Their horses' hooves echoed in the snow, the sound dull, muffled by the thick blanket of white that had settled over the land.

Kael had become accustomed to the cold. He had to. But tonight, the chill seemed to creep into his bones, settling deep, almost as if the land itself was trying to warn him. The air felt wrong, too still, like the calm before a storm.

Beside him, Seraphina rode in silence. Her pale-blue cloak swirled around her, and though her back was straight, her

27

hands, hidden by her sleeves, were clenched tight against the reins. Her eyes were focused on the horizon, the expression on her face unreadable. Even the light from the distant torches seemed to avoid her, as though it feared what she carried within.

Kael's gaze flickered to her, the intensity of her presence almost too much to bear. She was ice, and fire, and something else altogether. In the hours since their confrontation in her chambers, he had sensed the shift within her—her icy walls had cracked, just slightly, and he had seen the fear that she could no longer hide. But now, her demeanor had returned to the mask of the princess. Calm. Commanding.

Yet even with the distance between them, there was still a pull, something electric that neither could escape. Every glance, every unspoken word, seemed to intensify that attraction. It simmered just beneath the surface, a danger all on its own.

His horse's hooves dug into the snow as they descended into a hollow valley. The moon was full, casting long shadows over the frozen land, and the air hummed with a low, almost imperceptible vibration. Something was wrong.

He pulled his horse to a stop, his eyes scanning the area. The others followed suit, their faces tense beneath the pale moonlight.

"It's too quiet," one of the soldiers murmured, his voice barely more than a whisper.

Seraphina held up a hand, her posture rigid, as though she were listening to something far beyond the sounds of nature. "Move out," she said, her voice sharp, commanding.

Kael felt it before he saw it—an unsettling shift in the air, a ripple of magic far more familiar than he wanted to admit. His heart skipped a beat.

"Stay alert," he muttered under his breath, the fire within him stoking to life, just in case.

As they moved forward, the landscape around them began to change. The skeletal remains of a small outpost loomed in the distance, its stone walls half-crushed by the weight of time and neglect. It had once been a symbol of the border, a place of strength, but now it lay in ruin, the ashes of what had been a fire still smoldering on the periphery.

The smell of smoke was thick in the air. But this wasn't the kind of fire he was accustomed to—it was too cold, too still, as though it had burned with a controlled rage.

Seraphina's eyes narrowed as she dismounted, her boots crunching against the snow. Her movements were fluid, but there was a carefulness to them now. The ice around her, always there, seemed to pulse faintly, like the steady beat of her heart, but there was something about it tonight that felt… different. Something off.

Kael joined her, dismounting his own horse, his senses heightened. He scanned the area, searching for anything that didn't belong, and then he saw it. The mark—a deep gouge in the ground, almost like a symbol, drawn with blood, but the red wasn't fresh. It had been there for some time, hidden beneath the snow.

Seraphina stepped forward, her breath visible in the air, the frost in her veins responding to the scene before her. She knelt beside the mark, her fingers tracing the edges with a slow, deliberate motion.

"Do you see this?" she asked softly, though her voice was steady. "This is no ordinary attack. These marks… they're not from the Frostlands."

Kael bent low, examining the strange symbols etched into the earth. His brow furrowed. They weren't the symbols of the Ember Empire either. They were something older. Something far darker.

"No," he agreed, his voice tight. "They're not."

A low murmur spread through the soldiers as they began to circle the area, their eyes flicking nervously between the ruins and the sky. Kael's instincts screamed at him—danger was coming.

"What are we looking for, exactly?" one of the soldiers asked, his voice shaking slightly.

Seraphina stood up, her icy blue eyes fixed on the distance, as if she could see through the land itself. She was distant now, lost in a place Kael couldn't reach. "We're looking for the ones who did this. And we're looking for answers."

Her voice wavered only slightly, but Kael heard it. The vulnerability that she had so carefully hidden had bled through. She was afraid. And it wasn't just for her kingdom or for herself.

It was for something else. Something she couldn't control.

"Who would do this?" Kael asked quietly, his gaze still locked on the strange symbols. "Who would dare attack the Frostlands like this?"

Seraphina turned to face him, her lips pressed into a thin line. Her eyes met his, and for a moment, they were both lost in that space—caught in the dangerous gravity of what was unsaid between them.

"I don't know," she replied, her voice barely a whisper. "But I fear we're being manipulated. Someone wants us to fail."

Kael's heart skipped a beat, and the fire within him burned brighter. He had sensed it earlier, in the way she had closed herself off from him, in the tension that had gripped her during their ride. She knew something.

"You suspect someone," Kael said, his voice low and steady. "Who?"

Seraphina didn't answer immediately. She glanced around at the soldiers who were now speaking in hushed tones, their expressions shadowed by unease. The air was thick with the weight of uncertainty, and Kael could feel it, too.

Her gaze flickered back to him. "There are whispers of a rebellion. A faction within the Frostlands who believes our union with the Ember Empire is a betrayal. They would stop at nothing to prevent it."

Kael's thoughts raced. A rebellion? Within the Frostlands? That was far more dangerous than he had imagined.

"If this rebellion exists…" Kael began, his voice hardening, "Then they must be stopped before they destroy everything."

Seraphina's eyes darkened, the flicker of something ancient and wild swirling within them. "You think I don't know that? I've been doing everything in my power to keep the peace."

Kael took a step forward, closer than he'd intended, but the pull between them was too strong. "And yet, you still don't trust me."

The words were out before he could stop them. He regretted them immediately, but the truth had already been spoken.

Seraphina met his gaze, and for a long moment, the world seemed to fall away. There was no sound, no movement—just the two of them, standing amidst the ruins of a broken kingdom, their fates intertwined in ways they had yet to understand.

"I trust you, Kael," she said softly, though the words didn't seem to reach her eyes. "But I don't trust what's coming."

The quiet between them stretched, the tension like a taut rope, ready to snap.

Suddenly, the air shifted. A cold breeze swept through the ruins, carrying with it a whisper—a voice that was too distant to understand, but too close to ignore.

"Someone's here," Kael said, his voice urgent.

Seraphina's eyes widened. "Get back to the horses. Now."

Before Kael could respond, a shadow darted across the snow, too fast, too precise. He barely had time to react when the first arrow flew, its tip glinting in the moonlight.

The rebellion had come.

Six

Fire and Frost Collide

The moon hung heavy in the sky, casting its pale light over the ruins of the border outpost. Snow drifted lazily through the night air, swirling in gusts that carried the faint scent of smoke and ash. Kael stood at the edge of the destroyed fort, his breath fogging in the cold as his senses hummed with an awareness he couldn't quite shake. The ground beneath him still vibrated with the energy of the battle that had raged here, though it was now eerily silent. Too silent.

Around him, the soldiers were tense, their movements sharp, eyes scanning the horizon for any signs of attack. But it was the emptiness that unsettled Kael—the kind of emptiness that suggested they were being watched, their every move cataloged by eyes that could see far beyond the reach of mere mortals.

Seraphina stood to his left, her figure cast in shadow, her

hands hidden beneath the folds of her cloak. Even though she remained still, he could feel the currents of her magic rippling through the air, as subtle as the frost that clung to the earth beneath their feet. It was almost as if the entire world was holding its breath, waiting for something.

Kael knew that feeling well. He had felt it in the presence of danger, when the air became too thick to breathe, when every instinct screamed at him to run, yet his feet were rooted to the ground. Something was coming.

He turned to Seraphina, his gaze falling on her face, pale and drawn in the light of the fire burning in the distance. Her expression was unreadable, the mask she wore more impenetrable than ever. Her eyes, though—those ice-blue eyes—betrayed something. A flicker of uncertainty, a hint of fear that was barely contained beneath the calm exterior.

"Seraphina," he said, his voice low, though it carried the weight of his concern. "You don't have to do this. You can leave now. Go back to the palace. This is…" He paused, searching for the right word. "This is beyond you."

She turned her head to him, her lips pressing into a thin line. The wind caught a strand of her silver hair, pulling it across her face, but she didn't brush it away. Her gaze held his, steady, unyielding.

"You don't get to decide what's beyond me, Kael," she replied, her voice a mixture of steel and ice. "I am the princess of the Frostlands. These people are under my protection. You should remember that."

Kael opened his mouth to argue, but the words died on his tongue. He knew this. Knew she wouldn't back down. But he couldn't help himself. He couldn't stand the thought of her getting hurt. He had already seen too much of her strength to think she could be broken by anything—but what if?

His thoughts were interrupted by the sudden flash of movement at the far edge of the ruins. Kael's instincts kicked in immediately. Without thinking, he reached for Seraphina, pulling her back, his body shielding hers from whatever danger approached.

"Stay close," he murmured, his hand gripping her arm just a little too tightly. The warmth of her skin burned against his palm, and he forced himself to let go, though the ache in his chest lingered.

Seraphina's eyes met his, the briefest flicker of something passing between them. Something unspoken, yet understood.

Before Kael could react, the first of the attackers emerged from the shadows—dark figures in cloaks, their movements fast, fluid, and deadly. There were too many of them. Too many for their small group of soldiers to handle.

Kael's hand went to the hilt of his sword, his fingers tightening around the handle. The fire within him surged to life, crackling in his veins, ready to be unleashed. His body hummed with anticipation, but he kept himself in check. This wasn't the time to give in to the heat. Not yet.

Seraphina's hand brushed his arm, and for a moment, their gazes locked again. Her eyes were steady, but there was something—something darker—beneath the surface.

"Trust me," she said, her voice barely audible over the wind.

Kael nodded, though doubt gnawed at him. He had never fully understood her magic, and now was not the time to question it. Still, as he watched her step forward, her hands raising slightly, frost blooming from her fingertips, he couldn't shake the feeling that something had shifted in her. Something had changed.

The attackers charged, but as they neared, a blast of ice erupted from Seraphina's outstretched hand, freezing the ground beneath their feet. The rebels skidded to a halt, their momentum halted by the thick sheet of ice that formed in the blink of an eye.

Kael didn't hesitate. He rushed forward, his sword drawn, fire trailing behind him like a comet's tail. His blade cleaved through the air, a precise, deadly arc that took down two of the attackers in an instant. The heat from his fire surged with every strike, the flames licking the air, scorching anything in their path.

But even as the rebels fell, Kael's mind remained on Seraphina. She moved with a grace and power he had never seen before— frost swirling around her like a storm, her magic more precise, more controlled. More dangerous.

He had seen her fight before, but this was different. This was not just a defense of her kingdom. This was something personal. Something inside her had been unleashed, something raw, untamed.

He turned, but his attention snapped back to the battle as a figure lunged at him from the side. Without thinking, he raised his sword, blocking the strike just in time. The force of the blow pushed him back, his feet sliding in the snow. He could feel the heat from his sword sizzling against the cold air, the fire burning hotter now, almost out of control.

A shout pierced the chaos, and Kael's eyes flicked to Seraphina. She was surrounded. Several rebels had broken through her icy defenses, their weapons raised, ready to strike.

Without thinking, Kael surged forward, his body moving on instinct. He felt the heat of his magic rising, burning through him, but he couldn't stop it now. His fire roared to life, hot enough to melt the ice beneath his feet as he reached Seraphina.

He reached her just as one of the rebels raised a blade to strike. Without thinking, Kael thrust his sword forward, fire crackling through the air as he blocked the attack, sending the rebel sprawling backward.

"Seraphina!" he shouted, his voice rough with desperation. "Move!"

But she didn't. Instead, her gaze locked onto him, her eyes flashing with something he couldn't place. And then, without warning, she raised her hands, and the air around them seemed to freeze, locking everything in place.

The fire inside Kael sputtered, his magic responding to hers, but it wasn't right. It felt like his flames were being suffocated, smothered by the cold. Her magic was pulling him in, constricting him, and for a terrifying moment, Kael thought he might be lost in the storm she was conjuring.

Then, just as quickly, the magic released. The air snapped back into place, and the rebels that had surrounded them were frozen in their tracks, encased in ice from the tips of their weapons to the soles of their feet. The only sound was the wind, the crackling of ice, and the distant sounds of battle continuing elsewhere.

Kael exhaled sharply, his breath coming out in ragged gasps. He turned to Seraphina, who stood a few paces away, her chest rising and falling with the force of her breath. Her magic had drained her—he could see it in the way she swayed on her feet, the frost around her shimmering like an aura.

"What happened?" he asked, his voice tight. "You—"

"I didn't know it would happen like that," she interrupted, her voice distant. "I—I thought I could control it. But I…" She trailed off, her hands trembling as she lowered them to her sides.

Kael stepped toward her, reaching for her, his heart hammering in his chest. "Seraphina—"

Before he could reach her, a distant rumble shook the earth beneath their feet. A warning. The ground beneath them trembled, and Kael's eyes snapped toward the horizon.

"Get to the horses," Seraphina whispered, her voice hollow. "Now."

As they turned to leave, Kael's mind raced, but one thought kept echoing through his head, drowning out everything else: Something was wrong. They were not safe. Not here. Not anywhere. The forces working against them were not just enemies—they were something far older, far more dangerous.

And the worst part? Kael had no idea if their powers, their magic, could ever be enough to stop it.

Seven

A Moment of Weakness

The winds howled, cutting through the cracks of the stone walls like a thousand knives. Once a symbol of strength and invulnerability, the northern fortress now felt like a prison, its cold stone and ice-dusted halls a reminder that nothing, not even the strongest of walls, could keep the world at bay.

Kael sat at the edge of a large wooden table, his hands clasped tightly in front of him. His cloak was draped over the chair, the fire crackling low in the hearth, yet the warmth from the flames did little to chase away the chill that clung to him. His thoughts were a swirl of confusion and frustration, the ever-present weight of responsibility pressing on his shoulders. Each breath he took felt like it was punctuated by an unanswered question. What was happening here?

Seraphina had vanished earlier in the day, slipping away without a word. She had left behind only a faint trace of her magic—cold and distant, like an echo in the air that lingered long after her departure. This sudden retreat into silence was unlike her, and Kael found himself pacing the room, unable to focus on anything other than her absence.

A knock at the door pulled him from his thoughts.

"Come in," he called, his voice rough. He didn't even bother looking up as the door creaked open. It was not Seraphina, but one of the guards—a soldier who had accompanied them from the palace. The man's face was flushed with the cold, his eyes wide and filled with a quiet urgency.

"Prince Kael," the soldier began, his voice low, almost reverent. "It's the princess… She's not well."

The words struck Kael like a blow, his heart skipping a beat as he stood quickly, pushing the chair back with an audible scrape. "What do you mean? What's happened?" His voice was sharp with panic, a mixture of concern and anger at being kept in the dark.

The soldier swallowed hard before speaking again. "She… she's in her chambers. She's not responding. We've tried everything, but…" His words trailed off, leaving the unsaid hanging heavily between them.

Without another word, Kael spun toward the door, his boots thudding loudly against the stone floor as he rushed out of the room. The narrow corridors twisted and turned, each step echoing with the urgency building inside him. He had never seen Seraphina like this—unreachable, cold, distant. There was something more here, something deeper than just a simple illness, and his gut told him it had everything to do with the darkness they had uncovered in the ruins of the western outpost.

The fortress was quiet in the early hours of the morning, save for the distant howls of the wind, which seemed to seep through every crack in the walls. The guards saluted him as he passed, their faces stiff, wary of whatever might unfold, but none of them said a word. Kael didn't need to ask questions—he knew the way to her chambers by heart.

He reached the door to her quarters and stopped, his hand hovering over the handle. The very air felt heavy around him, charged with a tension that was impossible to ignore. He could feel her—could feel the ice that surrounded her like a storm cloud, and the low hum of her magic made his own fire stir, uneasy and unsettled.

"Seraphina," he said quietly, knocking softly, though the door was already half-open. His voice carried a layer of concern that he could no longer hide. His emotions, ever since that first meeting in the courtyard, had been raw, unpredictable, and now they felt as if they were threatening to consume him.

A faint rustle from inside reached his ears, but no response.

With a cautious breath, Kael pushed the door open.

The room was dimly lit by the flickering light of a single lantern. Seraphina lay motionless on the bed, her back to the door, her long, silver hair splayed across the pillow like a river of ice. The frost that seemed to follow her everywhere was thicker here, curling along the edges of the room, creeping over the floor, and coating the air in a fine mist.

"Seraphina?" Kael whispered again, his voice hoarse.

She didn't stir.

He stepped forward, the floor creaking beneath his weight. His instincts screamed at him to get closer, to reach her, but the frost in the air seemed to recoil from him as if warning him away. This wasn't normal.

Reaching the bed, he knelt beside her, his heart pounding as he gently touched her arm. The instant his skin made contact with hers, a shock of cold rushed through him, so sharp it nearly stole his breath.

"Seraphina!" he said, his voice more insistent now, his hand gripping her arm harder, his pulse racing. "You need to wake up."

Her eyelids fluttered, the faintest sign of movement, but she didn't open her eyes. She only murmured something, a word that was too soft for him to hear.

Kael leaned closer, his heart in his throat. "What did you say?"

Her lips barely parted. "It's not you… it's not you…" she whispered.

The words struck him with the force of a physical blow, and for a moment, his breath caught in his chest. Not you. Was she talking about him? The words felt like a dagger to the heart, and for a fleeting moment, Kael wondered if the cold in the room was more than just her magic—if the distance between them had grown too wide to bridge.

"Seraphina, look at me," he urged, his voice tight, desperate.

And finally, after what felt like an eternity, her eyes opened. They were glassy, distant, as though she were seeing something far beyond the walls of the room. Her gaze locked with his, and for the briefest moment, Kael saw something—a flicker of recognition, a hint of the woman he knew buried beneath the frost. But it was gone in an instant, replaced by something else.

"Why are you here?" she asked, her voice weak, barely more than a whisper.

Kael swallowed, his heart hammering in his chest. "I'm here because you're not well. You're not yourself." He searched her eyes, trying to find the Seraphina he had known, the strong, determined woman who had once commanded armies, who had stood tall and unyielding in the face of adversity. "What happened? What's going on?"

Seraphina shook her head, her lips trembling. "I can't… I can't control it anymore." Her voice cracked as if the weight of the words was too much to bear. "It's too much, Kael. The magic… the cold…" She squeezed her eyes shut, as if to shut out the world. "It's consuming me. I'm losing myself."

Kael felt his chest tighten, the air between them thick with something far heavier than cold. The raw fear in her eyes, the vulnerability she had never shown before, pierced him like a thousand shards of ice. She was afraid.

Before he could speak, she reached out, her fingers brushing his chest with a featherlight touch, sending a jolt of warmth straight through him. The contact was brief, but it left him breathless, his body responding to her like it had a mind of its own.

"I don't know what to do, Kael," she whispered. "I don't know how to stop it."

Kael's heart was pounding in his chest as he took her hand, gently pulling it away from his chest. His mind screamed at him to find the right words, to comfort her, to tell her that they would find a way through this, together. But as he looked down at her, her pale face streaked with tears, he realized something that sent a chill through his bones—he had no idea how to fix this. He had no answers.

"I won't leave you," he said, his voice low and steady, though he felt anything but steady. His words rang in the room like a vow, one he wasn't sure he could keep. "I promise, I won't leave you."

Seraphina's eyes softened for a moment, the frost around them flickering like a dying flame, but she didn't speak. She didn't have to. Her gaze said everything.

In the quiet of the room, with the storm raging outside and the weight of their unspoken truths hanging between them, Kael realized just how close they were to the edge—of everything.

Betrayal in the Shadows

The wind was sharper now, cutting through the narrow mountain pass like a blade, its chill creeping into Kael's bones despite the layers of fur he had bundled himself in. The stony cliffs rose high on either side, jagged and unforgiving, the snow beneath his boots crackling with every step. Each breath he took formed a mist that vanished into the air, disappearing as if it had never existed at all.

His mind raced, the cold biting at his skin doing little to numb the storm that brewed inside him. Betrayal.

The word echoed in his thoughts like a drumbeat, relentless and unyielding. It had been days since Seraphina had been taken, and still, the fear he had felt in that moment—the panic, the helplessness—clung to him like a shadow. They had been close, too close, to the truth. And now, someone in their midst had betrayed them. Someone had sent the rebels after them, had allowed Seraphina to be taken from the fortress.

Kael's hand tightened around the hilt of his sword, the familiar weight comforting, but also dangerous. His fire smoldered beneath his skin, hungry for release, but he knew that letting it burn too brightly here would only destroy everything around him. He had to keep control. He had to keep his mind sharp.

The cave they had been led to was dark, the air thick with the scent of damp earth and decay. A faint light flickered at the far end, casting long shadows along the walls. Kael moved forward cautiously, the faintest sense of unease crawling along his spine. The silence was oppressive, broken only by the sound of his breath and the distant drip of water from the ceiling. Every instinct in him screamed that something was wrong. The air felt too still, too suffocating.

Seraphina had been taken in the dead of night. A small group of rebels had stormed the fortress, cutting down the few guards who had been unlucky enough to be caught off guard. But the real shock had come when Kael discovered that the person who had been watching over her—the one who should have protected her—had been one of his own men. Someone close. Someone he trusted.

The betrayal stung more than the cold.

Kael's steps slowed as they reached the mouth of the cave, and he held up his hand to signal for the others to stop. His heart raced as he scanned the shadows, looking for any sign of movement. There, near the edge of the cave, a figure was standing motionless, half-shrouded in darkness.

"Seraphina?" Kael called, his voice rough with desperation.

At the sound of his voice, the figure stirred. It wasn't Seraphina. But it was someone he knew. Someone he never thought he'd see again.

"Jonas," Kael's voice dropped to a whisper, his heart hammering in his chest. "What are you doing here?"

Jonas, the lawyer who had once worked beside them, stepped forward from the shadows, his face illuminated by the flickering light. His expression was cold, unreadable, and his sharp features seemed to be carved from stone. The last time Kael had seen him, Jonas had been part of the counsel advising Seraphina. But now, there was something about him—something that Kael couldn't place—that made his blood run cold.

"I could ask you the same thing, Kael," Jonas said, his voice smooth, with a hint of amusement. "What brings the mighty prince of the Ember Empire to such a lovely place?"

The words felt like a mockery, and the amusement in Jonas's voice only deepened Kael's suspicion. He took a step forward, his gaze narrowing.

"Where is she?" Kael demanded, the fire inside him starting to stir. "Where is Seraphina?"

Jonas tilted his head slightly, as if considering the question. "She's fine," he said, but there was something in his tone that didn't sit right. "She's safe. For now."

Kael's heart lurched. "Safe? You think she's safe? You took her from the fortress. You betrayed us."

Jonas's lips curled into a slow smile, one that didn't reach his eyes. "Betrayed? I think you misunderstand. I didn't betray anyone. I've merely… seen things from a different perspective."

The words hung in the air between them, heavy with an unspoken threat. Kael's hand tightened around his sword, and his fire surged, eager to be released. But he held it back. He needed answers first.

"What perspective is that?" Kael asked through gritted teeth, stepping closer. "You think you can play this game? You think you can toy with the future of two kingdoms?"

Jonas's smile only deepened, but there was no warmth in it. "The future of two kingdoms is exactly why I'm here. Because there's something you don't see, Kael. Something Seraphina doesn't see. And it's time you both learned the truth."

Kael's heart skipped a beat. "The truth?" He took another step forward, his gaze narrowing. "What truth? What are you talking about?"

Jonas's gaze flickered to the shadows behind him, and Kael followed his glance, instinctively reaching for the hilt of his sword. But before he could react, a sound—a soft, almost imperceptible rustle—came from the far side of the cave. Kael's pulse quickened.

From the shadows, a second figure emerged, this one cloaked in darkness. The figure moved with a smooth, fluid grace, and Kael's instincts screamed at him that this was no ally.

The figure stepped into the light. The long, flowing cloak was a shade of deep crimson, and the face that emerged from beneath the hood was almost too familiar—Seraphina.

Kael froze, his breath caught in his chest. But it wasn't the Seraphina he had known. The woman before him was cold, distant, her eyes empty. The same eyes that had once held warmth now flickered with an unsettling emptiness. There was no recognition in them, no sign of the woman he had come to care for.

"Seraphina," Kael whispered, his voice breaking, a sudden lump forming in his throat. "What… what have they done to you?"

Her lips parted, but the voice that came from her was not hers. It was cold, flat, devoid of emotion. "I am the one you should be listening to, Kael. Not her."

Kael's heart clenched as his gaze flickered between Jonas and Seraphina, his mind racing, trying to piece together what was happening. What was happening to her?

Jonas stepped closer, a self-satisfied grin spreading across his face. "You see, Kael, you and Seraphina are just pawns in a much larger game. The balance between fire and ice… it's been manipulated for centuries. And now, it's time for that balance to tip."

Kael's mind reeled. "Manipulated? You're working with the rebels. You've been playing us this entire time."

Jonas nodded, his eyes gleaming with something far darker than Kael could have imagined. "More than that. I've been working for the true power behind this war. The one who controls both fire and frost. The one who will bring about the destruction of everything."

Kael's heart dropped. "You're not just working with the rebels," he said, the pieces clicking into place. "You're leading them."

Jonas's smile widened, his eyes gleaming with malice. "And now, Kael, you have a choice to make. You can join us, or you can watch everything burn. Because there's no stopping what's coming. The kingdoms will fall, and the prophecy will be fulfilled. Whether you like it or not."

Kael's chest tightened, his thoughts in a whirl. He looked to Seraphina, still standing like a statue, her expression unreadable. His heart twisted. He couldn't lose her. He couldn't let this happen.

He drew his sword, the fire within him flaring, but before he could take a step, the air around them shimmered. Seraphina's magic responded, her ice rising around them, freezing the ground in place. Kael's flames crackled in response, but the cold seemed to smother it, the clash between their powers shaking the cave.

"This is it, Kael," Jonas said softly, his voice the final strike. "The world will burn, or it will freeze. And you will have to decide which side you're on."

Kael's heart was heavy with the weight of his decision. In that moment, everything he had fought for—everything he had believed in—was slipping through his fingers. But he couldn't let go. Not now. Not when everything depended on him.

Nine

The Price of Power

The walls of the temple were ancient, the stone worn and cracked with the weight of centuries. Kael's footsteps echoed in the narrow corridor, the sound reverberating off the cold, damp walls, carrying an eerie sense of foreboding. The air was thick with the scent of moss and decay, the dim torchlight casting long, trembling shadows across the stone floor. He could feel the weight of the place pressing in on him—like the temple itself was alive, watching him, waiting.

Seraphina walked beside him, her expression unreadable, her pace slow and measured. She had been distant since the confrontation with Jonas, her mind seemingly consumed by thoughts Kael could not reach. He had tried to talk to her, to break through the wall of ice she had erected around herself, but each time she withdrew further into herself. And the longer they walked through this forsaken place, the more Kael feared that something within her had already been lost.

The temple was silent, save for the soft hiss of Seraphina's breath, and Kael could hear the faintest tremor in it, as though she were holding herself together by sheer will alone. He wanted to reach out, to offer comfort, but the distance between them seemed insurmountable. It's not just the ice. He knew it was more than that. It was the magic—the weight of the prophecy—and whatever secrets Jonas had hidden from them. Whatever they had uncovered about her powers, about the forces that had been manipulating them from the shadows.

Kael glanced at her, but she didn't look back. Her eyes were focused straight ahead, fixed on something far beyond the walls of the temple, her gaze distant and unfocused.

"Seraphina," Kael said, his voice softer than he intended. "We can still stop this. Whatever Jonas has planned—whatever he's told you… we can still fight back."

Seraphina's eyes flickered, but she didn't answer immediately. She only took another step forward, her boots making a muted sound on the stone floor. Kael's heart twisted. He couldn't stand the distance between them, couldn't stand how the woman he had come to care for seemed to be slipping through his fingers, like water, no matter how hard he tried to hold onto her.

They came to a large chamber at the heart of the temple. The ceiling soared high above them, supported by thick stone pillars that seemed to stretch into the shadows. In the center of the room stood an altar, its surface covered in ancient symbols, long faded but still visible in the flickering torchlight. The air around the altar felt charged, thick with magic—old magic, dark magic.

Seraphina stepped forward, her breath coming faster now, as though the very presence of the altar was pulling something out of her. Kael's pulse quickened as he watched her, unsure of what she was about to do.

"Seraphina," he called again, but his voice was swallowed by the vastness of the chamber.

She didn't respond, her fingers reaching out to touch the stone of the altar. The moment her hand made contact, the air seemed to shimmer, the temperature dropping sharply, and Kael felt a shiver crawl up his spine. The frost in the air thickened, swirling around them like a storm, and for the first time, Kael felt a twinge of fear.

Seraphina's eyes closed, her face tight with concentration, and for a moment, she seemed to lose herself in the depths of whatever magic she was channeling. Kael stepped closer, his heart pounding, his instincts screaming at him to stop her, to pull her away from the altar. But something held him back, something darker than just fear.

"You don't have to do this," he said, his voice thick with urgency. "This is a trap. They want you to—"

"I have no choice, Kael," Seraphina interrupted, her voice raw, edged with pain. "I've already made my choice."

The words hit him like a physical blow, and he staggered back, the weight of them crashing into him with the force of a storm. She had made her choice? What did that mean? Did she mean that she had already chosen the path Jonas had shown her? Had she truly turned away from him, from everything they had fought for?

Kael's thoughts were a whirl of confusion and panic, but before he could speak, the temperature in the room plummeted further, the cold seeping into his bones, freezing the words in his mouth. Seraphina's hands were now pressing flat against the altar, her head bent as though she were listening to something only she could hear.

Kael's fire stirred within him, flickering like a candle struggling against the wind. He took a step forward, his boots crunching against the frost-covered floor. "Seraphina," he said, his voice hoarse. "Look at me. Please."

But she didn't respond. Her face was pale, her lips parted as though she were breathing in something, something he couldn't feel. The power in the air was thick, suffocating, and the shadows seemed to deepen around them.

Then, the voice—low, almost a whisper—filled the room.

"Do you feel it?" the voice asked, soft as the wind. It came from Seraphina, but it was not hers. The words were not hers. "The power within you, Seraphina. The magic that calls to you, that begs you to embrace it. You are the key to everything."

Kael's blood ran cold. The voice was not Seraphina's. It was something older, something darker.

He reached for her, his fingers grazing her wrist, and as soon as his skin touched hers, the world seemed to tilt. The room spun, the air becoming thick with energy, and for a moment, Kael couldn't breathe. The magic in Seraphina surged, a force so powerful that it threatened to pull him under, to drown him in a wave of cold and heat all at once.

"Stop!" he shouted, his voice breaking through the haze. "Seraphina, stop!"

But her eyes remained closed, her body stiff, as though she were trapped in a trance. The voice continued, its words seeping into Kael's mind, filling him with an unease he couldn't shake.

"You think you can control it, Kael? You think you can save her? But she is not yours to save. She belongs to something far greater."

Kael's heart pounded in his chest. The voice was speaking of Seraphina, but it was speaking of something else—something far darker than he had imagined. He could feel the magic swelling within her, thrumming like a living thing, like a beast caged inside her. He didn't know how much longer he could hold on, how much longer he could keep himself from losing control.

"Seraphina," he pleaded, his voice raw. "Please, listen to me. Don't let this destroy you."

Her eyes snapped open, but they weren't the eyes he recognized. They were empty, cold—like the frozen lake that had once been her home. There was nothing of Seraphina left in them.

"You don't understand," she said, her voice distant. "I never wanted this. But I don't have a choice. This is the only way to stop it."

"To stop what?" Kael demanded, his chest tightening with panic. "Stop what?"

"The destruction," she whispered, her voice cracking. "The world will burn, or it will freeze. And I can't stop it, Kael. I can't control it anymore."

The words sent a jolt of ice through him, a chilling realization washing over him. Seraphina was not just fighting for control over her own powers—she was fighting something else. Something far bigger, far more dangerous than either of them had imagined. And it was controlling her.

"Seraphina," Kael said, his voice breaking. "You don't have to do this. You're not alone. We can fight this together."

Her gaze flickered to him, and for a brief moment, he saw something—something human, something familiar—in her eyes. But then it was gone, replaced once more by the cold, empty stare of the stranger standing before him.

"I'm sorry, Kael," she whispered. "I've already made my choice."

Before he could stop her, the magic within her erupted, sending a shockwave through the room. Kael was thrown backward, his body crashing into the stone wall. The power surged, overwhelming him, filling the air with a suffocating pressure that left him gasping for breath.

And in that moment, Kael realized the truth—there was no escaping this. The price of power had been paid, and neither of them could ever go back.

Ten

Fire Against Ice

The cave was suffocating. The air was thick with the clash of magic—the heat of Kael's fire, the biting cold of Seraphina's ice—swirling around them in a dizzying dance of opposing forces. Each breath Kael took felt like it was fighting against the freezing air, but the fire within him burned hotter, stronger, every second. The walls of the ancient cavern groaned under the weight of their struggle, the sound muffled by the growing storm between them.

Kael's heart thundered in his chest as he stood facing Seraphina. The space between them felt like a chasm, one that no amount of fire could bridge. His eyes locked onto hers, but there was nothing in them—nothing of the woman he had once known, the woman who had stood beside him in the face of danger, their magic entwined in a bond stronger than anything he had ever known.

Now, all that remained was the cold.

The wind howled, the cave shuddering under the power of their magic, and Kael could feel his fire battling against the ice in the air. It was like standing in the eye of a storm, where everything he had known about control, about balance, was slipping away with every heartbeat.

"Seraphina," he said, his voice thick with both pain and desperation. "Please, stop this. Let me help you. I can still reach you. We can fight together."

Seraphina's gaze flickered for the briefest moment, but her expression remained unchanged. The chill in the air deepened, pressing against Kael's chest like a weight he couldn't escape. The icy barrier she had raised between them was impenetrable. Her eyes were distant, unfocused—like she wasn't truly seeing him.

"Kael," she whispered, her voice barely audible beneath the roar of the storm. "You don't understand. You don't know what this is. You can't help me."

The words cut through him like a blade, and Kael felt the fire within him flare up, almost violently, as though it wanted to burn everything around him. His body was alive with heat, with urgency, but it was out of his control. It was too much.

"You're wrong," he said through clenched teeth. "I understand more than you think. I see what you're doing. You think this is the only way. But it's not, Seraphina. I'm right here. Let me help you."

Seraphina's eyes flickered, and for the briefest moment, Kael thought he saw something there—a crack in the ice, a flicker of the woman he knew. But just as quickly, it was gone, swallowed by the cold.

"I can't stop it, Kael. I can't control it anymore," she said, her voice shaking. Her hands were raised before her, her fingers trembling slightly, though the ice around her remained absolute. "This power… it's too strong. And I'm too weak."

Kael's pulse quickened, and his fire surged in response to the anguish in her voice. He could feel it now—her fear. She was terrified, not just of the power within her, but of what it was turning her into. He could see it in the way she held herself, the way she distanced herself from him.

The cold was not just a physical barrier. It was a wall she had built around her heart, one that Kael couldn't break, no matter how hard he tried.

"Seraphina," he said softly, his voice breaking as he took a step forward, unable to stop himself. "I know you're afraid. I know you think you're alone in this. But you're not. You're not alone. We're in this together, always."

Her eyes finally met his, and for the first time in what felt like forever, Kael saw something flicker in the depths of them. It was brief, like a shadow passing over water, but it was enough to make his heart ache. She was still there. She was still the woman he had fought beside, the woman he had come to care for in ways he couldn't name.

The tension in the air grew, the battle between their powers swirling in a chaotic storm around them. Kael could feel the heat of his fire trying to break through, trying to wrap around her, to soothe her, to pull her from the darkness that had taken hold of her. But it couldn't reach her. Not yet.

"I don't know how to stop this," Seraphina said, her voice cracking with emotion. She was shaking now, her hands falling limply at her sides. "I don't know if I even want to anymore."

The words stung more than Kael cared to admit. She was giving up. She was surrendering to the very thing that terrified her. And he couldn't let her do that.

"You're stronger than this," Kael said, his voice a low growl of determination. "You've always been stronger than this. Don't let them win, Seraphina. Don't let this power define you."

For a moment, it seemed like the world held its breath. The wind stopped howling, the air grew still, and all Kael could hear was the beating of his own heart, the steady rhythm that told him there was still time.

Seraphina's expression softened, just for an instant. Her eyes shimmered with unshed tears, and Kael saw the vulnerability in her, the raw fear that had been buried beneath the ice. She was struggling—struggling to hold on to the last piece of herself, the last shred of who she had been before all of this.

And Kael realized, with a terrible clarity, that this wasn't just about her power, or about the battle between fire and ice. This was about something much deeper. Something that went beyond magic. This was about trust. Trust between them. Trust that they could fight this together.

But as the air grew colder still, a creeping doubt slithered into his mind. What if she couldn't hear him? What if she was too far gone?

"Please," he whispered, his voice thick with emotion. "I need you. We need you."

Seraphina closed her eyes, her chest rising and falling with uneven breaths. She looked almost as if she were listening to something that only she could hear. Her fingers twitched, and Kael held his breath, waiting for some sign, any sign, that she was returning to him.

Then, with a sharp intake of breath, Seraphina raised her hands again, and the cold intensified.

"Seraphina!" Kael shouted, his voice rising with panic. He took a step forward, but the magic in the air pushed him back, the walls of fire threatening to collapse in on themselves.

But she didn't seem to notice. Her eyes remained closed, her expression strained. "I'm sorry, Kael," she whispered, her voice barely audible over the storm. "I can't stop it. I can't stop this darkness inside me."

In that moment, Kael realized the truth: she had given up. She had given herself over to the power, to the darkness, and there was nothing he could do to stop it. The warmth of his fire seemed to dissipate, swallowed by the frost that had consumed her.

But Kael refused to let go. Not yet.

He moved toward her again, through the ice, his hand outstretched, his voice a plea. "Please, Seraphina… Don't do this. Don't let it win."

The magic crackled, a violent storm of fire and ice that collided between them, and for the briefest moment, Kael thought he might lose her. But then, something shifted. The fire surged in him, pulsing with life and heat, and suddenly, he could feel her. Her warmth. Her light. It was still there.

Seraphina gasped, her eyes snapping open as the ice around them cracked. The magic was still swirling, but now it was different—less cold, less suffocating. Her hands trembled, but the ice in her veins seemed to retreat, slowly, unwillingly.

"You're not alone," Kael whispered, stepping closer, his hand finally reaching for hers.

And in that moment, as their magic collided—fire against ice— Kael knew this battle was far from over. But it wasn't just a battle against each other. It was a battle for her soul.

Eleven

A Love That Burns

The fortress had fallen silent after the storm. The walls, once humming with the energy of battle, now stood still, echoing with the weight of the past. The cold was biting, like needles in the air, and it clung to Kael's skin even though the fire within him still raged. His magic—untamed, fierce—was still alive, but something had changed.

Seraphina's power, her ice, was still there, still filling the air between them like an invisible barrier. But now, it wasn't the suffocating cold it had been before. There was something different in the way the frost danced around them. It was no longer a war between their forces—it was a fragile truce, held together by something both dangerous and beautiful.

He could feel her. The warmth of her presence was unmistakable, even though she stood across the room from him, her back to the fire. Her hair fell in silvery strands around her face, the soft glow of the hearth catching in the wisps of frost that still clung to her skin.

Kael's heart twisted as he watched her. Her eyes were closed, her breath coming slow and steady. She looked so peaceful, almost as if she had found a moment of respite from the storm inside her.

But Kael knew better than to believe in quiet peace. He could feel the storm still brewing in the depths of her soul, a tempest that threatened to break free at any moment. It was a storm they had both been fighting, ever since the prophecy had begun to unravel.

It had been days since they had emerged from the cave, days since the magic had nearly consumed them both. They had traveled back to the fortress together, but even now, after all they had been through, they hadn't spoken much. The weight of their unspoken words hung between them like a specter, and Kael couldn't help but wonder if there was a way back from the edge they had both teetered on.

"Seraphina," Kael said softly, his voice breaking the silence. His words felt heavy, like stones falling into a still lake. "Can we talk?"

Her shoulders tensed at the sound of his voice, and for a long moment, she didn't respond. Her eyes remained closed, her face expressionless.

"I know you're not asleep," Kael said, stepping closer. "I'm not going to leave until we talk."

Seraphina's lips parted, and for a moment, Kael thought she was going to speak, but instead, she turned her head slightly, her gaze fixed on the fire. Her face was shadowed, but the pale light revealed the strain in her expression.

"There's nothing more to say, Kael," she whispered. "I've made my choice. This is who I am now."

Kael felt his heart tighten at her words. He had known the distance between them was growing, but hearing it spoken aloud was like a punch to the gut. He had thought they had come through the worst of it. He had thought they were finally on the same side, that they could move past the darkness that had torn them apart. But now...

"You don't mean that," Kael said, his voice soft but insistent. He stepped closer, his boots scraping softly against the stone floor. "I can see it in your eyes. I know you, Seraphina. You're not ready to give up on everything."

Her head snapped toward him, her eyes flashing with an intensity that made his chest constrict. There was fire in those eyes—ice and fire, both battling within her.

"Don't tell me what I feel," she said, her voice low, dangerous. "You don't understand. You think you do, but you don't. You think you can save me, that you can change everything, but you can't. I can't even save myself."

Kael's heart ached, a sharp, searing pain that cut through him. He knew she was pushing him away. She was afraid—afraid of what the magic was doing to her, afraid of what it had turned her into. But he couldn't stand to see her like this. He couldn't stand to see her breaking apart.

"I don't need to save you," Kael said, his voice thick with emotion. "I just need you to let me in. Let me help you. Whatever this is, we can face it together. We've already been through hell, Seraphina. We've come this far. Don't push me away now."

Seraphina's eyes softened for the briefest moment, but it was enough to make Kael's pulse race. She was still there. She was still the woman he had come to care for, the woman whose fire and frost had once been in perfect balance. He could see it now, the small flicker of the woman he loved fighting against the ice that had consumed her.

"I'm scared," she whispered, her voice breaking. "I don't know what's happening to me. I don't know if I can control this anymore. What if I hurt you, Kael? What if I lose myself in it completely?"

Kael took another step forward, the heat from his body reaching out to her, even though the air around them was still cold, still thick with the remnants of their magic. He reached for her hand, his fingers brushing against her cool skin. The touch was tentative, fragile, but it was enough. He could feel the electricity that passed between them, the pull that had always been there, even when they had been torn apart.

"I'm not going anywhere," Kael said, his voice steady, even though the storm inside him threatened to overwhelm him. "I'll never leave you. You're not alone in this. We can fight it together. We can find a way."

Seraphina's lips parted as if she were about to say something, but then she stopped. Her gaze dropped to their hands, still resting together, and for a moment, the room seemed to hold its breath.

"I don't know if I can stop it, Kael," she said, her voice barely above a whisper. "I'm afraid. I'm afraid of what I'll become. Of what I've already become."

Kael felt his heart break at the words, but he knew one thing with certainty—he couldn't lose her.

"Then let me be your strength," Kael said, his voice fierce, the fire within him flaring in response to her fear. "Let me fight with you. Whatever you are, whatever you're becoming, I'll be there. I'll stand by you. We don't have to do this alone. You're not alone, Seraphina. I love you. And I'll keep fighting for you, no matter what."

Seraphina's breath caught in her throat, and for a moment, the world seemed to hold still. Her eyes searched his face, the rawness in them mirrored in his own. The ice around them had begun to crack, but the fire was still there, burning bright between them. And in that moment, Kael realized something— he didn't need to save her. She wasn't some fragile thing to be fixed. She was strong, and together, they could face whatever came next.

"I love you too," Seraphina whispered, her voice barely audible, but the words were clear, cutting through the air between them.

The world seemed to fall away in that instant. The ice, the fire, the magic—they all disappeared, leaving only the two of them standing there, hands entwined, their hearts beating as one. It was a fragile moment, a delicate balance of fire and ice, but it was enough. For now, it was enough.

"I won't let you go," Kael said, his voice fierce with conviction. "We'll face it together. I'll fight by your side, no matter the cost."

Seraphina's eyes softened, the cold retreating from them, replaced by something warmer. Something human. Something real.

For the first time in what felt like forever, Kael saw the woman he had come to care for—truly see her, not just the magic or the cold—but the person she was. And in that moment, he knew they could overcome anything, as long as they had each other.

The storm between them had not ended, but they had found a way to fight it together.

For now, that was all they needed.

Twelve

Frosted

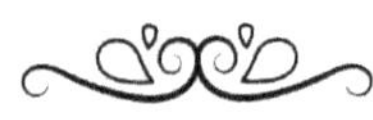

The castle stood bathed in the soft light of dawn, the sky above a pale, muted gray. The first rays of sunlight streaked across the horizon, painting the snow with shades of gold and lavender, but the light could not chase away the cold that gripped the land. The winds still howled through the battlements, whipping up the snowdrifts that covered the paths and the watchtowers.

Kael stood on the balcony of the royal tower, his gaze lost in the swirling storm below, the chill of the morning seeping into his bones. His fingers drummed restlessly against the stone railing, though the warmth of the fire within him pushed back against the icy air. The cold was nothing compared to the chill inside him, the gnawing unease that had been building ever since the night they had shared their vows, when Seraphina had promised that they would stand together.

But they hadn't. Not truly.

His eyes flickered to the door behind him. The heavy wood remained closed, and though Kael had left it ajar, Seraphina had not come to join him. She hadn't come to speak with him in days, though they shared the same space, though they slept in the same bed. He could still feel the warmth of her presence, the imprint of her in the sheets beside him, but the silence between them was suffocating.

They had fought the forces trying to tear them apart, fought the rebels, the darkness creeping inside of her. And yet now that they had won, now that they had taken the first steps toward peace, it felt like they were at an impasse.

He wanted to believe that things could go back to the way they were—that they could find their way together again. But it wasn't that simple. **It couldn't be.**

He turned away from the balcony, the frost on the stone beneath his boots crackling softly as he crossed the room. The door was still closed, and the silence was deafening. His hand hovered over the handle for a long moment, unsure of what to do, but before he could turn it, he heard her voice.

"Kael."

The voice came from behind him, so soft, so tentative that he almost missed it. His heart skipped a beat as he turned to find Seraphina standing in the doorway. She was framed by the dim light of the hallway, her figure silhouetted by the glow from the torches that lined the walls. The frost that still clung to her skin shimmered in the candlelight, but there was something different in the way she stood now. She was no longer the woman consumed by the cold, no longer the ice queen she had been. But there was something else in her eyes—a distance, a wariness—that made Kael's chest tighten.

She looked at him, her eyes dark and unreadable. For a long moment, neither of them spoke. Kael could feel the weight of the words that had been unspoken between them for days.

"Seraphina," he finally said, his voice rough with emotion. "I… I don't know where we stand anymore."

Her gaze flickered, and she stepped further into the room, her boots leaving soft marks in the frost that had accumulated on the stone floor. She stopped a few feet away from him, her hands clasped in front of her, her shoulders tense.

"I don't know either," she said, her voice barely above a whisper.

Kael's heart sank. He could feel the distance between them growing, like an unbridgeable chasm. "I've tried to be patient, Seraphina. But we can't keep pretending that everything is fine.

We've been through too much for this silence."

The room felt colder as he spoke, the air thickening with the weight of his words. Seraphina's eyes dropped to the floor, and for a moment, Kael thought she might turn away. But instead, she looked up again, her gaze locking onto his, steady and unflinching.

"It's not just silence," she said, her voice quiet but firm. "It's the fear, Kael. The fear that I'll lose myself again. That I'll become someone else, someone I don't recognize."

Kael's pulse quickened, his hands clenching at his sides. He could feel the fire in him rising again, the heat surging in his chest. But he fought to keep it under control, to stay calm, to reach her. He couldn't lose her. Not now.

"I'm not afraid of what you've become," Kael said, his voice softer now, full of the weight of his own emotions. "I'm afraid of losing you. The person you are, Seraphina. I don't care about the magic. I don't care about the power inside you. I care about you. I always have."

She looked at him then, her eyes softening for the first time in days. It was a fleeting moment, but it was enough. Enough to make Kael's heart skip in his chest, enough to remind him of what they had fought for.

"I'm afraid of losing myself too," Seraphina whispered, her voice trembling. "I don't know who I am anymore, Kael. I've been running from the ice, running from the fire inside me, and now it feels like I'm trapped between the two. I can't… I can't find a way out."

Kael took a step forward, his heart pounding in his chest. "You don't have to find your way out alone. We've been through hell, Seraphina. Together. And I'm not going anywhere. You don't have to fight this by yourself."

She shook her head, the motion slow, unsure. "I don't know if we can do this. Not anymore. I've already been changed by the power. What if it's too late for me? What if we're too far gone?"

The words cut through him like ice, but Kael refused to let them bury him. He couldn't lose her, not like this. He reached for her then, his hands trembling slightly as he cupped her face, his thumb brushing across her cheek, the warmth of his touch stark against the coolness of her skin.

"I won't let you go," he said, his voice low, fierce with determination. "We're both changed by the power inside us. But it doesn't define us. We define who we are, Seraphina. Together."

Her breath caught, and for a moment, Kael thought she might pull away, but instead, she leaned into his touch, her eyes fluttering closed. The warmth of her skin against his palm was a comfort he hadn't realized he needed. He could feel the flicker of her magic beneath the surface, but this time, it wasn't cold. It wasn't suffocating. It was like the first spark of fire, just beginning to light the darkness.

When she opened her eyes again, they were filled with something new—uncertainty, yes, but also a spark of hope. The frost that had held her captive seemed to melt, just a little, under the warmth of his touch.

"I'm scared," Seraphina admitted, her voice barely a whisper. "I'm scared of what I might do, of what might happen if I lose control again. But I don't want to be alone in this anymore."

Kael's heart swelled with something too big to name, something that was part relief and part love, burning bright and pure between them. He stepped closer, wrapping his arms around her and embracing her. Her breath hitched in his chest, and

Kael could feel the tension in her body, the weight of her fear. But beneath it, there was something else. A willingness to try, to trust him again. To let go of the ice, if only for a moment.

"I'm not going anywhere," Kael whispered against her hair. "I'll be here, Seraphina. I'll always be here."

For a long moment, they stood together, their bodies pressed close, the warmth of their magic swirling between them. The ice that had once kept them apart was beginning to melt, slowly, but surely, the first signs of thawing. And in the warmth of their shared magic, Kael realized something—**they were not alone.** They had each other.

And that was enough.